PEARSON
GUIDE TO
RESEARCH
NAVIGATOR™
2009

UPPER SADDLE RIVER, NEW JERSEY 07458

©2009 by PEARSON EDUCATION, INC.
Upper Saddle River, New Jersey 07458

10 9 8 7 6 5 4 3 2 1

ISBN 10: 0-205-63340-4
ISBN 13: 978-0-205-63340-1

Printed in the United States of America

Note: Research Navigator™ is continually expanded and updated. The screen shots included in this documentation may not reflect the latest updates. Refer to <http://www.researchnavigator.com/phguide/> to download the most recent documentation in either Microsoft® Word format or Adobe Acrobat® format.

Contents

iii

Quick Guide to Research Navigator™

To Register

From your Internet server log on to: www.researchnavigator.com

- Click "Register" under new users on the left side of the homepage screen.
- Enter the access code exactly as it appears on the inside front cover of this guide.
- Follow the instructions on screen to complete your registration—you may click the Help button at any time if you are unsure how to respond.
- Once you have successfully completed registration, write down the Login name and Password you just created and keep it in a safe place. You will need to enter it each time you want to revisit Research Navigator™.
- Once you register, you have access to all the resources in Research Navigator for twelve months.

What Is Research Navigator™?

Research Navigator™ is designed to help you with the research process, from identifying a topic to editing the final draft. It serves as an ideal starting point for your research and offers guidance on how to make your trips to the campus library more productive.

Research Navigator™ includes four databases of credible and reliable source material to get your research process started:

1. The EBSCO/ContentSelect Academic Journal and Abstract Database, organized by subject, contains many of the leading academic journals for each discipline covered. Instructors and students can search the online journal by keyword, topic, or multiple topics. Articles include abstract and citation information and can be cut, pasted, e-mailed, or saved for later use.

This site is perfect for academic research papers where professional journals and scholarly reference articles are required. For instance, you are required to write a paper on the latest research regarding global warming. Using the ContentSelect Database, you might pull up articles from publications such as *Environmental Science, Scientific American, Geographic and Atmospheric Science, Political Science Quarterly,* or *Science, Technology, and Human Value.*

2. A link to *The New York Times* is provided on Research Navigator's homepage. *The New York Times* has recently opened their full-text archive of content from 1981 to the present. To search for *New York Times* content on any subject, simply follow the link to www.nytimes.com.

This site is a great place to see how the concepts you are studying apply to the real world. For instance, perhaps you are studying the topic of constitutional law. By searching the *New York Times* database you would uncover articles written about right-to-life cases and the legality of banning gay marriages.

3. Link Library, organized by subject, offers editorially selected "Best of the Web" sites. Link Libraries are continually scanned and kept up-to-date, providing the most relevant and accurate links for research assignments.

Better than an open-access search engine, using Link Library/The Best of the Web links you to editorially reviewed and credible websites. It saves you valuable time by allowing you to search only sites that have been pre-selected by instructors around the country. Perhaps you have been assigned a project on affirmative action. The Best of the Web will quickly get you to sites like *American Association for Affirmative Action, National Organization for Women, and The Affirmative Actions and Diversity Project.*

4. The *Financial Times* Archive and Company Financials provides a searchable one-year archive and five-year financials for the 500 largest U.S. companies (by gross revenue).

Perfect for researching all things business, the *Financial Times* Archive gives you one place to get the best in business news. Whether you are researching a company's portfolio for a class or just investigating it for a future career, this database gives you the information you need quickly.

Research Navigator™ is simple to use and easy to navigate. The goal is to help you complete research assignments or research papers quickly and efficiently. The site is organized around the following sections (identified by tabs):

- Home
- The Research Process
- Finding Sources
- Using Your Library
- Start Writing
- Endnotes & Bibliography

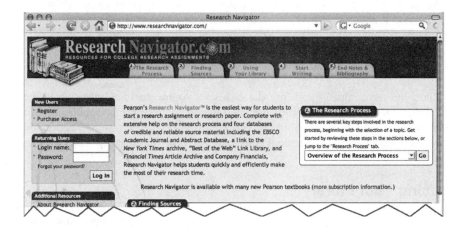

Research Navigator™ Tabs

From Research Navigator™'s homepage, you can have easy access to all of the site's main features including a quick route to the four databases of source content.

The Research Process

Here you will find extensive help on all aspects of the research process including:

- Selection of a Research Topic
- Establishing a Research Schedule
- Creating Effective Notes
- Research Paper Paradigms
- Understanding and Finding "Source" Material
- Understanding and Avoiding Plagiarism

Once you have selected and narrowed your research topic, you are now ready to gather data. Gathering data is a serious task. Some leads will turn out to be dead ends; other leads will provide only trivial information. Some research will be duplicated, and a recursive pattern will develop; that is, you will go back and forth from reading, to searching indexes, the Internet, the library, and back again to reading. One idea modifies another until you begin discovering connections and refining your topic even further.

Finding Sources

Research Navigator™ simplifies your research efforts by giving you a convenient launching pad for gathering data. The site has aggregated four distinct types of source material commonly used in research assignments; academic journals (EBSCO's ContentSelect), newspaper articles (a link to *The New York Times*), World Wide Web sites (Link Library), and business news data (*The Financial Times*). For in-depth help in using ContentSelect, Link Library, and the *Financial Times* archive, see Chapters 2-4 of this guide.

Once you have mined these four databases for source material, move on to the detailed information on how to use the Internet for research assignments, also included in this *Finding Sources* tab. Finish by reviewing the section on primary sources, such as personal conversations, e-mails, interviews, or surveys.

Using Your Library

After you have selected your topic and gathered source material from the four databases of content on Research Navigator™, you may need to complete your research by going to your school library. Research Navigator™ does not try to replace the library, but rather to help you understand how to use library resources effectively and efficiently.

You may put off going to the library to complete research assignments or research papers because the library can seem overwhelming. Research Navigator™ provides a bridge to the library by taking you through a simple step-by-step overview of how to make the most of your library time. Written by a library scientist, the *Using Your Library* tab explains:

- Major types of libraries
- What the library has to offer
- The role of the librarian
- Using library catalogs
- Using websites for research
- Using electronic databases
- Finding print materials including texts, magazines, etc.
- How to choose the right library tools for a project
- How to make the most of research time in the library

In addition, when you are ready to use the library to complete a research assignment or research paper, Research Navigator™ includes 31 discipline-specific "library guides" for you to use as a roadmap. Each guide includes an overview of the discipline's major subject databases, online journals, and key associations and newsgroups. Feel free to print them out, and take them with you to the library!

Start Writing

Once you have become well acquainted with the steps in the research process and gathered source materials from Research Navigator™ and your school library, it is time to begin writing your assignment. Content found in this tab will help you do just that, beginning with a discussion on how to draft a research paper in an academic style.

Other areas addressed include:

- Blending reference material into your writing
- Writing the introduction, body, and conclusion
- Revising, proofreading, and formatting the rough draft

You will also find sample research papers for your reference. Use them as a guide to writing your own assignment.

A newer addition to this tab is an online **Grammar Guide**. Its content spells out some of the rules and conventions of standard written English. Included are guidelines and examples for good sentence structure; tips for proper use of articles, plurals and possessives, pronouns, adjectives and adverbs; details on subject-verb agreement and verb tense consistency; and help with the various forms of punctuation.

Endnotes & Bibliography

The final step in a research assignment is to create endnotes and a bibliography. In an era dubbed "The Information Age," knowledge and words are taking on more significance than ever. Laws requiring writers to document or give credit to the sources of information, while evolving, must be followed.

Various organizations have developed style manuals detailing how to document sources in their particular disciplines. For writing in the humanities and social science, the *Modern Language Association* (MLA) and *American Psychological Association* (APA) guidelines are the most commonly used, but others, such as those in *The Chicago Manual of Style* (CMS), are also required. The purpose of this Research Navigator™ tab is to help you properly cite your research sources. It contains detailed information on MLA, APA, CMS, and CSE styles. You will also find guidance on how to cite the material you have gathered from this Research Navigator™ site!

You may also elect to use the new **AutoCite** feature. It is designed to assist you in the creation of a "Works Cited" or "References" document to accompany your research assignment. You may refer to the detailed examples provided in this section's various style guides, or you may use **AutoCite** to document a source in either MLA, APA, or CMS format. Simply enter the title of your research project, select one of the three documentation styles, and then click on "Add a New Source." Once you've saved your source, this and all prior entries for this project title will be displayed should you need to make changes to or delete a source. A printer-friendly version of your listings is also available.

Now, you are ready to go! Please let us know your experiences with Research Navigator. Contact us at: research_navigatorservice@pearsonhighered.com

Chapter 1

Introducing
Research Navigator™

What Is Research Navigator
and How Can It Help with Research?

Research Navigator is an online academic research service that combines four major databases with practical research assistance—all in one place on the Web. It can help you understand the steps in the research process while also providing in-depth information on conducting library research.

Research Navigator offers these databases of credible and reliable source material: EBSCO's ContentSelect Academic Journal and Abstract Database, a link to the *New York Times* archive, the *Financial Times* Article Archive and Company Financials, and the "Best of the Web" Link Library. It also guides students step-by-step through the writing of a research paper. Access to Research Navigator is free with the purchase of any Pearson Education college textbook.

To begin using Research Navigator, register with the personal access code found in this guide. Once you register, you have access to all the resources in Research Navigator for six or twelve months, depending on your text.

What's in Research Navigator?

From the homepage, you can gain access to all of the site's main features, including the four databases—for academic journals and general interest publications (EBSCO's ContentSelect), newspaper articles (a link to the *New York Times* archive and the *Financial Times* Article Archive), financial data (the *Financial Times* Company Financials), and World Wide Web sites ("Best of the Web" Link Library)—that will be discussed in greater detail later. If you are new to the research process, you may want to start by browsing "The Research Process," located in the upper right-hand section of the homepage. Here you will find help on all aspects of conducting research, from finding a topic to creating effective notes, research paper paradigms, and avoiding plagiarism.

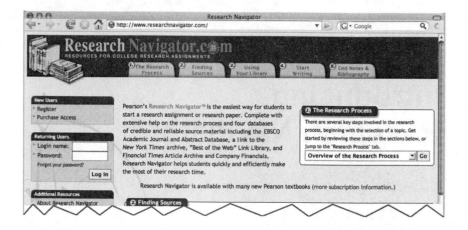

ContentSelect

EBSCO's ContentSelect Research Database gives you instant access to thousands of academic journals and periodicals from any computer with an Internet connection.

When you need the most authoritative take on a subject, especially one that is complex or very specialized, you will turn to academic journals. Academic journals are aimed at a professional audience—researchers, instructors, and experts, usually affiliated with colleges and universities. Academic-journal articles have been peer-reviewed before publication; that is, experts in the field have checked them for balance, methodology, and significance. An article that doesn't meet the profession's standards will not be published in an academic journal. Examples of academic journals are *Science, Nature, American Ethnologist, Journal of Chemical Education*, and *Canadian Journal of Sociology*.

When you do a search, your list will include some results in full-text format. The full article may be in HTML, the common language used to write Web documents, or it may be in a PDF format. PDF is a file format that creates high-resolution documents; to read such documents, however, you need to first download a free viewer, Adobe Acrobat Reader.

Many ContentSelect results will be in a citation format; when you click on those results, you will get a bibliographic reference with author, subject, and journal source. A citation will usually contain an abstract, or brief summary of the article, that will help you determine whether you want to find the full article. You then find the full article through the journal's online archive, or in a print or electronic version through your college library's catalog.

To use ContentSelect, select a database to search and then enter a keyword. For more detailed information, see Chapter 2.

Link to the *New York Times* Archive

Among daily newspapers, *The New York Times* is the gold standard. It is widely considered the nation's newspaper of record because it is comprehensive and staffed by reporters and editors who are experienced and well regarded. It has substantial resources and a tradition of excellence. The *Times*, however, like other newspapers, is aimed at a general audience and is limited by daily deadlines, competitive pressures, and space, so individual articles may not be suitable sources for a complex or very specialized research topic. But for day-to-day coverage of events and popular issues, and general, accessible background information on a wide range of topics, it is first rate.

A link to *The New York Times* is provided on Research Navigator's homepage. *The New York Times* has recently opened their full-text archive of content from 1981 to the present. To search for *New York Times* content on any subject, simply follow the link to www.nytimes.com

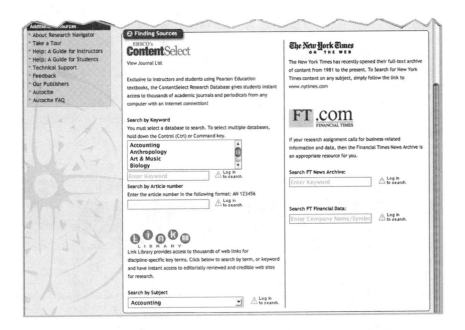

Link Library

Link Library is a collection of links to websites, organized by academic subject and key terms. To use this database, select a subject from the drop-down list. You will be taken to a list of key terms; find the key term for your subject and see a list of five or more editorially reviewed websites that offer educationally relevant and credible content. The Web links in Link Library are monitored and updated each week, reducing your chances of encountering dead links. For more detailed information, see Chapter 3.

The *Financial Times* Article Archive and Company Financials

There may be instances when your research assignment calls for business-related information and data. Through an exclusive agreement with *The Financial Times*, a leading daily newspaper covering national and international business, you can search a one-year archive of news stories affecting companies, industries, and economies. Also use this database to access five-year financials for the 500 largest U.S. companies (by gross revenue). For more detailed information, see Chapter 4.

Other Resources within Research Navigator

Using Your Library

Despite the Internet revolution, a visit to a bricks-and-mortar library continues to be an important part of the research process. Use the drop-down list on the Research Navigator homepage "Using Your Library" tab to select a "Library Guide" for your subject. The guide will list Library of Congress and Dewey call numbers, major print and online journals, organizations and associations, discussion lists, and Internet resources. Print it out and take it with you to help you navigate a library's vast resources more efficiently.

"Using Your Library" also discusses types of libraries, their resources, how to choose which ones to use, and the research process and how to develop a timeframe for it.

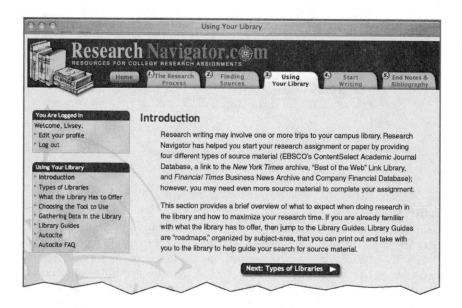

Start Writing

Once you have become acquainted with the steps in the research process and gathered source materials from Research Navigator and your school library, it is time to begin writing your assignment. Content found in this tab will help you do just that, beginning with a discussion on how to draft a research paper in an academic style. Other areas addressed include:

- Blending reference material into your writing
- Writing the introduction, body, and conclusion
- Revising, proofreading, and formatting the rough draft

This is also the tab where you will find sample research papers for your reference. Use them as a guide to writing your own assignment.

A newer addition to this tab is an online **Grammar Guide**. Its content spells out some of the rules and conventions of standard written English. Included are guidelines and examples for good sentence structure; tips for proper use of articles, plurals and possessives, pronouns, adjectives and adverbs; details on subject-verb agreement and verb tense consistency; and help with the various forms of punctuation.

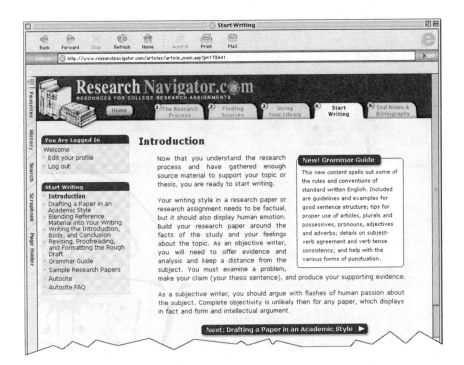

Endnotes & Bibliography

The final step in a research assignment is to create endnotes and a bibliography. In an era dubbed "The Information Age," knowledge and words are taking on more significance than ever. Laws requiring writers to document or give credit to the sources of information, while evolving, must be followed.

Various organizations have developed style manuals detailing how to document sources in their particular disciplines. For writing in the humanities and social sciences, the Modern Language Association (MLA) and American Psychological Association (APA) guidelines are the most commonly used, but others, such as those in *The Chicago Manual of Style* (CMS), are also required. The purpose of this Research Navigator™ tab is to help you properly cite your research sources. It contains detailed information on MLA, APA, CMS, and CSE styles. You will also find guidance on how to cite the material you have gathered right from this Research Navigator site!

You may also elect to use the new **AutoCite** feature. It is designed to assist you in the creation of a "Works Cited" or "References" document to accompany your research assignment. You may refer to the detailed examples provided in this section's various style guides, or you may use **AutoCite** to document a source in either MLA, APA, or CMS format. Simply enter the title of your research project, select one of the three documentation styles, and then click on "Add a New Source." Once you've saved your source, this and all prior entries for this project title will be displayed should you need to make changes to or delete a source. A printer-friendly version of your listings is also available.

Chapter 2

Using ContentSelect

About ContentSelect

EBSCO's ContentSelect Academic Journal Database is an archive of scholarly peer-reviewed journals and general interest periodicals. Thousands of articles and citations from general interest publications and prestigious academic journals can be instantly accessed in several ways using ContentSelect's search engine. Titles are chosen to reflect multiple perspectives in a range of topics, under 31 broad subject headings in the sciences, humanities, and social sciences.

Of course, ContentSelect is not a substitute for evaluation. Careful research studies sometimes contradict one another, and even authorities disagree. However, while many sources on the Internet may present questionable data or rely on dubious authorities to draw conclusions, ContentSelect provides a wealth of professionally-reviewed information that you can search and evaluate with confidence.

What's in ContentSelect?

ContentSelect offers searchable databases of academic journals and general interest publications. Academic journals are peer-reviewed; general interest publications are not.

Academic Journals
Rather than having a staff of writers who write something on assignment, journals accept submissions from academic researchers all over the country and the world. The journal editor then relies on "peer reviewers," or experts in the author's field, to evaluate the papers submitted to help determine if they should be published. The result is that the content of journal articles meets a higher standard than that of popular magazines, newspaper articles, or Web pages. Journals provide specialized knowledge and information about a research topic and adhere to strict professional guidelines for methodology and theoretical grounding.

Scholarly journals are published several times per year. All the issues published in one calendar year constitute a volume. For example, the *American Sociological Review*, the journal of the American Sociological Association,

7

published Volume 69 in the year 2004. That year's volume was made up of six individual issues, numbered Vol. 69 No. 1, and so on.

Additionally, journal issues may contain letters to the editor, book reviews, and comments from authors.

General Interest Publications

In addition to scholarly journals, subject databases—particularly the General Interest database—in ContentSelect include periodicals that are not peer reviewed. Some examples are *Commentary, Washington Monthly, Newsweek, USA Today Magazine,* and the *Christian Science Monitor.* These publications are included because they have articles that are generally credible and reliable. If your topic is timely or controversial, general interest publications may offer more appropriate coverage than academic journals.

Sometimes it's not easy to know at first glance which category a publication fits. For example, you find an article in *Science News.* Is that an academic journal, as the journal *Science* is? Once you've conducted a search in your subject database, click on the "publications" tab at the top of your results page. You can scroll down to *Science News* or use the "browse" button to find it. When you click on *Science News,* you'll get an information box that describes the subjects it covers plus a characterization of its content: "presents articles of interest to scientists and others ..." The "and others" is a clue; then, when you check the "peer reviewed" section, it has an "N" for "no." So *Science News* is a general interest publication, not an academic journal. Still, any article in *Science News* is probably reliable, subject to the evaluation you conduct for all sources.

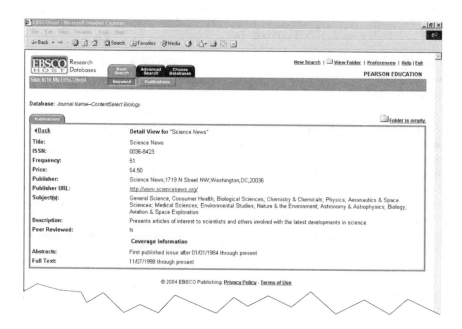

Searching ContentSelect

Select a Database

ContentSelect's homepage features a list of databases. To search within a single database, click the name of the database. To search in more than one database, hold down the alt or command key while clicking on the name of the database.

Basic Search

After selecting one or more databases, you must enter a keyword or keywords, then click on "go." This will take you to the basic search window. If you've selected a precise and distinctive keyword, your search may be done. But if you have too many results—which is often the case—you need to narrow your search.

Standard Search (Boolean)

- **And** combines search terms so that each result contains all of the terms. For example, search **SUV and conservation** to find only articles that contain both terms.
- **Or** combines search terms so that each result contains at least one of the terms. For example, search **SUV or conservation** to find results that contain either term.
- **Not** excludes terms so that each result does not contain the term that follows the "not" operator. For example, search **SUV not conservation** to find results that contain the term **SUV** but not the term **conservation.**

Using the above examples, suppose you were writing a paper about sport utility vehicles and energy conservation, in light of growing criticism of their low gasoline mileage. If you selected the "General Interest" database from ContentSelect and used the Boolean "or," at the time this was written, you would get 800 results for **SUV or conservation**. If you used the Boolean "and" option, (**SUV and conservation**) you would get only two results:

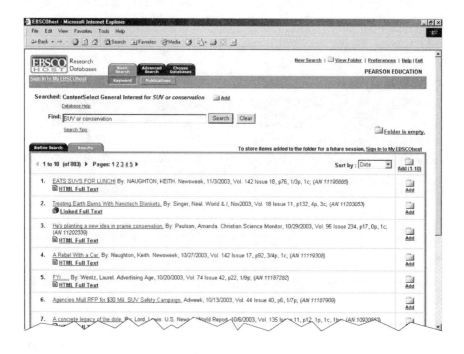

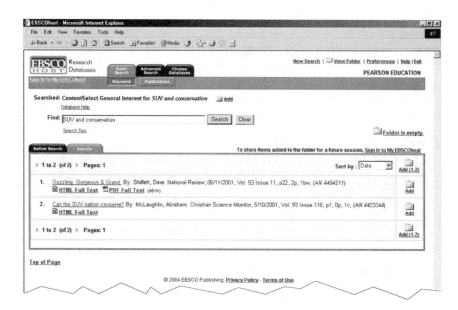

But suppose you decided to write about SUVs and didn't want articles that mentioned the energy conservation issue. If you searched for **SUV not conservation**, you would get 194 results:

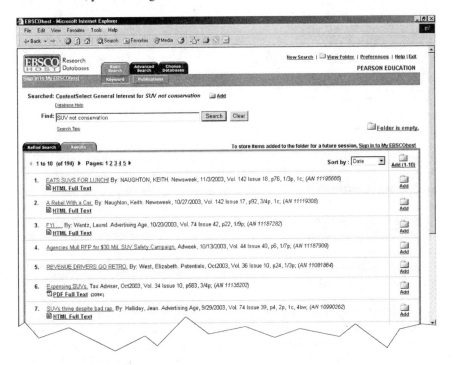

Search by Article Number
Each and every article in the EBSCO ContentSelect Academic Journal and Abstract Database is assigned its own unique article number. In some cases, you may know the exact article number for the journal article you would like to retrieve. Perhaps you noted it during a prior research session on Research Navigator. Such article numbers might also be found on a Companion Website for your text, or in the text itself.

To retrieve a specific article, type the article number in the "Search by Article Number" field and click the **GO** button.

Advanced Search
On the tabbed tool bar, click **Advanced Search**. The advanced search window appears. Enter your search terms in the **Find** field. Your search terms can be keywords or selections from search history. Boolean operators (AND, OR, NOT) can also be included in your search.

You can also use **field codes** with your search terms. Fields refer to searchable aspects of an article or Web page; in the case of ContentSelect, they include author, title, subject, abstract, and journal name. Click **Field Codes** to display a list of field codes available with the databases you are using. Type the field code before your search terms to limit those words to the field you entered. For example, **AU Naughton** will find records that contain Naughton in the author field.

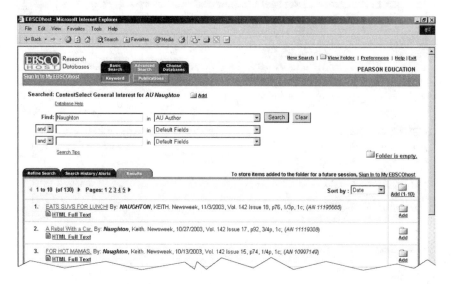

To **print**, **e-mail**, **or save** several search results, click on the folder next to the result; then print, e-mail, or save from the folder at the top of the results field. (You can still print, e-mail, or save individual results from the open article or citation.)

You can remove specific results, or clear the entire folder and collect new results, during your session. If you end your session, or it times out due to inactivity, the folder is automatically cleared.

Full Text Results

Some ContentSelect results will be available in full text—that is, if you click on the full text logo at the bottom of an entry, you will be able to call up the entire journal or magazine article. If you want to limit your search to results available in full text, click on the "search options" tab, and then on "full text." Then renew your search.

Abstract and Citation Results

Many ContentSelect results are in the form of citations containing abstracts. A **citation** is a bibliographic reference to an article or document, with basic information such as ISSN (International Standard Serial Number, the standard method for identifying publications) and publisher that will help you locate it. An **abstract** is a brief description of an article, usually written by the author. An abstract will help you decide whether you want to locate the work—either in an electronic database or a print version—through your college library.

A handy tip: once you have found an article that meets your research needs, you can search fields easily from the article citation to turn up similar articles. For example, suppose the *Christian Science Monitor* article "Gas-guzzling SUVs muster up a makeover" (Evarts, July 6, 2000) suits your paper perfectly. Go to the citation and click on the subject field to find similar articles. Or, if you want to see what else the author has written, click on the author field to produce a list of articles he has written.

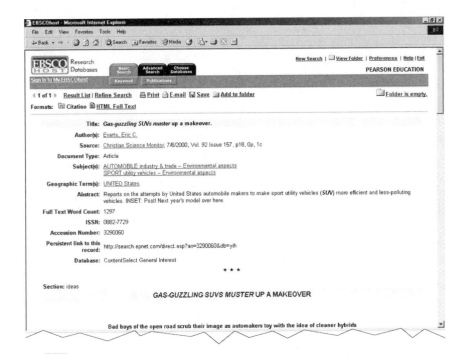

In many cases you can search the full text of articles using electronic databases and then read the entire article online. Typically, in order to use these databases you need to have a library card number or special password provided by the library. But sometimes when you use an electronic database you will find that the text of an article won't be accessible online, so you'll have to go to the library's shelves to find the magazine or newspaper in which the article originally appeared.

For more information, explore the "Using Your Library" tab on the Research Navigator homepage.

Chapter 3

Using Link Library

Link Library and the Web

Link Library is a collection of Web links, organized into 37 academic subjects, which are in turn divided into subcategories and lists of individual sites. The sites are editorially reviewed, which means that they have been selected because they offer credible and reliable information.

For example, if you were to select the "pollution" subcategory from the **Biology—Environmental Science** subject category, you would get a list of a dozen links. The site topics range from different types of pollution—air, noise,

15

water—to the status of environmental legislation. How dependable are the sources? All are well-known and well-regarded government or educational institutions: the Environmental Protection Agency, NASA Ames Research Center, the University of California at Irvine. Some may quarrel with policies and enforcement efforts of government agencies, but the federal government has a long-established role in collecting data and disseminating information. The government websites listed here cover straightforward, non-controversial subjects: a definition of water pollution, how stratospheric ozone is being depleted, the latest city-by-city air pollution data, etc.

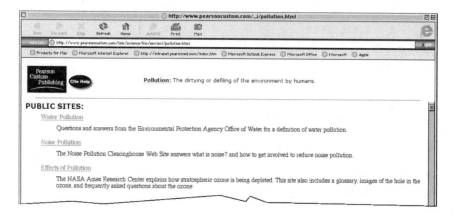

Suppose you look for the same information from websites listed by Yahoo! It turns out that many sites listed under "pollution" are from government and educational agencies. But you will also come across sites like one in which the author describes herself as "devoted to addressing the aspects of the environmental crisis left unacknowledged or inadequately addressed by the vast majority of existing environmental groups." The site is attractive, it doesn't solicit contributions, and it collects articles from generally well-regarded secondary sources, like the Associated Press. But its focus is on opinion, and lists topic headings such as "prophecy" and "prayer." It contains little of scholarly interest and no discernible research evidence. The site's author, while enthusiastic and well-intentioned, is not well-known or well-regarded.

In addition, the Web links in Research Navigator's Link Library are monitored and updated each week to reduce the chance of encountering "dead" links.

What's in Link Library?

Link Library echoes the variety of the World Wide Web. It offers images, text, government and academic documents and research, databases, and search engines. As with any subject directory, you need to narrow your search to the most useful category. You can find links to websites about AIDS, for example, in a half-dozen subject categories: biology, criminal justice, U.S. and world history, philosophy-ethics, and sociology. When you have selected a subject area and found the topic you are seeking, you will find a list of sites. The character of the site you choose to consult will often depend on your topic. The sites in Link Library can be:

- **Scholarly.** If you are researching photosynthesis and you go to the **Biology** subject area, you will find such sites as "What Is Photosynthesis?" and "Photosynthesis Research," maintained by Arizona State University. "Virtual Chloroplast," by the University of Illinois at Urbana-Champaign, contains an image of a chloroplast that lets you click on certain regions for more information.

- **Straightforward.** What if you want information on the 2004 presidential election? Go to **Political Science – American Government > Presidential Elections**. It has sites such as "Atlas of U.S. Presidential Elections," with voting results for elections dating back to 1860; "U.S. Electoral College," the homepage for the National Archives and Records Administration Guide to the Electoral College; and "Elections," which provides graphs on electoral and popular votes for all U.S. presidential elections to date.

- **Controversial.** You're researching a topic that has heated arguments on both—or many—sides, and you want to summarize the range of public opinion. Link Library subject directories on such topics will lead you to a balanced variety of voices. Under **Philosophy–Ethics**, for example, you will find a list of "partial-birth abortion" links that include a pro-choice site, the text of the *Roe vs. Wade* decision, the National Right to Life Committee homepage, a site that attempts to provide all views of the issue, and a Planned Parenthood site that describes medical procedures performed at various stages of pregnancy.

- **Practical.** Want some help in finding sources on the Web? Go to the **Information Technology** subject directory. The "search engine" heading offers tips for effective Internet searching, common questions about how search engines work, and a chart to help you choose the best search engine for a task.

Finding Information with Link Library

To use this database you choose a subject from the drop-down list, and, using the alphabetical directory, find the key term for the topic you are searching. Click on the key term and see a list of editorially reviewed websites.

Some topics with wide-ranging aspects appear under more than one subject heading. For example, a list of websites about alcoholism and alcohol abuse can be found under Criminal Justice, U.S. History, General Psychology, and Sociology.

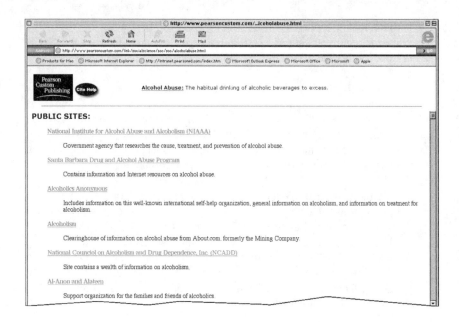

http://www.pearsoncustom.com/link/socialscience/soc/soc/alcoholabuse.html

Products for Mac | Microsoft Internet Explorer | http://intranet.pearsoned.com/index.htm | Microsoft Outlook Express | Microsoft Office | Microsoft | Apple

Pearson Custom Publishing Cite Help

Alcohol Abuse: The habitual drinking of alcoholic beverages to excess.

PUBLIC SITES:

National Institute for Alcohol Abuse and Alcoholism (NIAAA)

Government agency that researches the cause, treatment, and prevention of alcohol abuse.

Santa Barbara Drug and Alcohol Abuse Program

Contains information and Internet resources on alcohol abuse.

Alcoholics Anonymous

Includes information on this well-known international self-help organization, general information on alcoholism, and information on treatment for alcoholism.

Alcoholism

Clearinghouse of information on alcohol abuse from About.com, formerly the Mining Company.

National Council on Alcoholism and Drug Dependence, Inc. (NCADD)

Site contains a wealth of information on alcoholism.

Al-Anon and Alateen

Support organization for the families and friends of alcoholics.

Chapter 4

Using the
Financial Times Article
Archive and Company
Financials Database

Also included in Research Navigator™ is the ***Financial Times* Article Archive and Company Financials Database**. Through an exclusive agreement with the *Financial Times*, a leading daily newspaper covering national and international business, you can search this publication's one-year archive for news stories affecting companies, industries, and economies. Simply enter your keyword(s) in the text box and click the **GO** button.

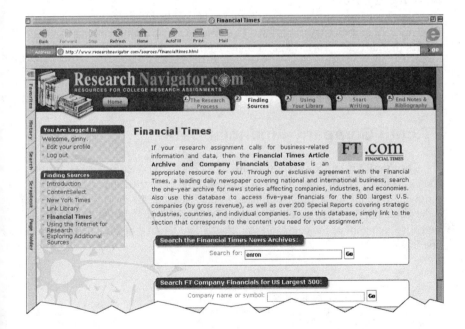

Search by Keyword

"And" Behavior

By default, the search engine only returns pages that match all of the keywords entered in a search query. The more keywords you use, the more refined the search becomes. There is no need to type the word "**and**" between keywords, as this is done automatically by the search engine.

Case Sensitivity

The Search engine does not differentiate between upper and lower case. A search for dna, DNA, or dNa will all return pages containing the keyword "DNA".

Searching Within Results

Often a first attempt at searching produces too many search results. To narrow the results, you may want to perform a new search that searches only within the results returned by the too-broad search query. This is often called "narrowing a search" or "searching within the current search results." To narrow a search, all you need to do is add more words to the end of your query. This give you a new query that will return a subset of the pages returned by the too-broad query.

Sorting by Date

The *Financial Times* article archive sorts article results by relevance, with the most relevant stories appearing first. To view the most recently published articles first, use the "Sort by" pull down menu located just above the search results.

FT.com Company Financial Data

The **Company Financials Database** offers access to five-year financials for the 500 largest U.S. companies (by gross revenue). To view the financial data for a company, type the name of the company in the "**Search**" field. If the company name you enter does not match a company in this database, you will see a results page displaying all of the companies in the top 500 list that begin with the same first letter.

Balance sheet summary

Year ended:	31-Dec-02 USD	31-Dec-01 USD	31-Dec-00 USD	31-Dec-99 USD	31-Dec-98 USD
Investment Properties	-	-	-	-	-
Other Property	(876m)	(707m)	(419m)	(324m)	(302m)
Other Tangible Fixed Assets	3,272m	2,903m	2,910m	2,741m	2,577m
Tangible Fixed Assets	**2,396m**	**2,196m**	**2,491m**	**2,417m**	**2,275m**
Intangibles	**12,460m**	**14,121m**	**13,526m**	**16,225m**	**16,442m**
Financial Assets	**1,140m**	**646m**	**467m**	**537m**	**550m**
Fixed Assets	**15,996m**	**16,963m**	**16,484m**	**19,179m**	**19,267m**
Stocks	2,032m	2,177m	1,908m	1,950m	6,850m
Debtors	4,539m	4,613m	5,220m	6,751m	1,694m
Cash & Equivalents	544m	1,214m	871m	230m	421m
Assets Held For Resale	-	-	-	-	-
Current Assets	**7,190m**	**9,647m**	**8,013m**	**8,931m**	**8,965m**
Total Assets	23,946m	26,773m	26,777m	28,110m	28,232m

Avoiding Plagiarism and Documenting Your Electronic Sources

What Is Plagiarism?

It is plagiarism to present another person's words or ideas as if they were your own. A kind of theft, plagiarism can result in failing a course or even in expulsion from college. While blatant, intentional plagiarism is not the campus norm, many students fail to fully understand what constitutes plagiarism. Internet research in particular poses pitfalls: information can be copied from the Web with the click of a mouse, and too many students wrongly believe that anything on the Internet is in the public domain. Others believe that they can escape detection because a professor couldn't read all the possible sources on a topic; however, instructors can now access websites that scan documents and search the Internet to identify plagiarized material.

The most flagrant forms of plagiarism are the use of another student's work, the purchase of a "canned" research paper, or knowingly copying passages into a research paper without documentation. Sometimes students unintentionally plagiarize through carelessness—by leaving off quotation marks or failing to document sources properly. Also, too many students believe that merely changing sentence order or a few words in a passage avoids plagiarism.

Using Copyrighted Materials

Just as a patent protects an inventor's rights to exploit a new product, a copyright signifies original creation and ownership of written words, music, or images. As a student, you may use copyrighted material in your research paper under the doctrine of fair use, which allows the use of others' words for such informational purposes as criticism, comment, news reporting, teaching, scholarship, or research. Copyright law is not intended to halt the flow of ideas and facts; it is meant to protect the literary, musical, or visual form that an author or artist uses to express his concepts. Academic integrity requires documenting such use in the manner covered in this appendix. If you use substantial blocks of material, or you want to download images for your paper, you should seek permission from the author or website. When in doubt, consult your instructor or e-mail the author or another contact for the Internet site.

How to Avoid Plagiarism

Always credit the source for any ideas and words not your own. That said, a fear of plagiarism should not force you to document the obvious. You do not have to document common knowledge—information that most educated people know. (For example, that George W. Bush did not win the popular vote in the 2000 presidential election is common knowledge; a newspaper citation would be unnecessary.) You also do not have to document your own thinking, including points or conclusions that you have reached through the course of your research.

Paraphrasing

When you paraphrase, you restate *in your own words* a passage written or spoken by another person—and no more. Your writing should reflect the original passage's emphasis in your own phrasing and sentence structure. Compare the following passages. Here's the original, from a Stanford University website on South Africa:

> With the enactment of apartheid laws in 1948, racial discrimination was institutionalized. Race laws touched every aspect of social life, including a prohibition of marriage between non-whites and whites, and the sanctioning of "white-only" jobs. In 1950, the Population Registration Act required that all South Africans be racially classified into one of three categories, white, black (African) or colored (of mixed descent). The colored category included major subgroups of Indians and Asians. Classification into these categories was based on appearance, social acceptance and descent. For example, a white person was defined as "in appearance obviously a white person or generally accepted as a white person." A person could not be considered white if one of his or her parents were non-white. The determination that a person was "obviously white" would take into account "his habits, education and speech, and deportment and demeanor" (Chokshi, Carter, Gupta, Martin, & Allen, 1991).

Unacceptable Paraphrase (underlined words are plagiarized):

> · According to Chokshi et al. (1991), racial discrimination was institutionalized with passage of the apartheid laws in 1948. Race laws touched every aspect of social life, including banning marriage between races, and the sanctioning of "white-only" jobs. The 1950 Population Registration Act required that all South Africans be racially classified as white, black (African) or colored (of mixed descent, Indian or

24

Asian). Classification <u>was based on appearance, social acceptance and descent</u>. A white person, for example, was "in appearance obviously a white person or generally accepted as a white person." <u>A person could not be considered white if one of his parents were non-white</u>. According to the act, determining <u>that a person was "obviously white" would take into account</u> "his habits, education and speech, and deportment and demeanor."

In the above example, citing the authors (Chokshi et al., meaning "Chokshi and others") at the beginning does not legitimize using the authors' exact wording — nor does changing a few words and the order of phrases.

Acceptable Paraphrase:

The 1948 apartheid laws made racial discrimination official. The wide-ranging laws allowed "white-only" jobs and banned marriage between races. Two years later, the Population Registration Act classified all South Africans into one of three racial categories: white, black (African) or colored. "Colored" South Africans were of mixed descent or were Indians or Asians. According to Chokshi et al. (1991), the categories were determined by "appearance, social acceptance and descent." An officially "white" person, then, had been judged to look like a white person or was accepted as one. A white person could not have a non-white parent. The act posited that "habits, education and speech, and deportment and demeanor" would help determine the classification.

Here, the writer has borrowed two phrases from the original, but enclosed them in quotes or attributed them properly—to Chokshi et al. and the Population Registration Act.

Summarizing

A summary condenses the essentials of someone else's thought into a few statements. A summary is shorter than a paraphrase and provides only the main point from the original source. Keep it short; a summary should reduce the original by at least half. As with a paraphrase, keep your own ideas and opinions separate; you may want to note them to yourself and use them elsewhere in your paper, however.

Here is how the above quotation could be summarized:

The 1948 apartheid laws institutionalized racial discrimination in South Africa, affecting all aspects of social life. The 1950 Population Registration Act set up three categories of races, determined by such factors as appearance and descent (Chokshi, Carter, Gupta, Martin & Allen, 1991).

Quoting Sources

Enclose within quotations marks all quoted materials—a phrase, a sentence, a paragraph. (Some documentation styles specify that if you are quoting more than a sentence or two, the quote should be indented instead and set off typographically.) Don't load a paper with quotations; if more than a quarter of your essay consists of quotations, you are letting others speak for you and giving the impression that you have not synthesized the material. When drawing from an authority, rely mostly on paraphrase and summary. *Do* use a quotation, however, when it fits your message and its language is particularly on point or if the idea is hard to paraphrase accurately.

> Diane Sollee (1996), the founder and director of the Coalition for Marriage, Family and Couples Education, said, "The number one predictor of divorce is the habitual avoidance of conflict."

Quote exactly; if you drop a quoted phrase within a sentence, make sure the grammar meshes with your own. If you eliminate a sentence or words within the quote, use ellipses according to the appropriate documentation style.

> Halberstam (2001) described "… a dramatically changed America, one which has been challenged by the cruelest kind of terrorism, and which is in a kind of suspended state between war and peace …and where so much of our normal agenda has been brushed aside."

How to Include Reference Citations in Your Text

As you take notes, keep meticulous track of your sources. You may want to print a hard copy of each Web article used in order to save the author or authors, organization, title, date, and URL for later reference—especially since Web pages are created and taken down constantly. When you cite electronic sources, it is vital to type every letter, number, symbol, and space accurately. Any error makes it impossible to retrieve your source.

Find out which documentation standard your instructor is using. The major styles used are MLA (Modern Language Association), APA (American Psychological Association), CMS (Chicago Manual of Style), or CSE (Council of Science Editors, formerly the Council of Biology Editors).

Guidance for all of these styles may be found on the Research Navigator homepage (www.researchnavigator.com) at the "End Notes & Bibliography" tab (Tab 5). You may refer to the detailed examples provided in this section's various style guides, or you may use **AutoCite** to document a source in APA, MLA, or CMS format. Simply enter the title of your research project, select one of the documentation styles, and then click on "Add a New Source." Once you've saved your source, this and all prior entries for this project title will be displayed should you need to make changes to or delete a source. A printer-friendly version of your listings is also available.

American Psychological Association (APA) Style

The American Psychological Association (APA) style is generally used in the social sciences. The most recent (5th) edition of the *Publication Manual of the American Psychological Association* provides guidelines for citing electronic sources:

American Psychological Association. (2001). *Publication manual of the American Psychological Association* (5th ed.). Washington, DC: Author.

The APA has published specific examples for documenting Web sources on its Web page: http://www.apastyle.org

In writing an APA-style research paper, you must use in-text citations, set in parenthesis, to document your sources. Identify the source by the author and the copyright year. For example:

People from the Mediterranean prefer elbow-to-shoulder distance from each other (Smith, 1998).

At the end of your paper, you must provide a list of your sources, with complete information, in a "References" section. In using APA style to document your electronic sources, all references begin with the same information that would be provided for a printed source (or as much of that information as possible). The Web information is then placed at the end of the reference. It is important to use the "Retrieved from" and the date because documents on the Web may change in content, move, or be removed from a site altogether.

See the Research Navigator homepage (www.researchnavigator.com) at the "End Notes & Bibliography" tab for guidance in setting up your APA-style "References" section.

Modern Language Association (MLA) Style

The Modern Language Association (MLA) style is widely used in the humanities. For general information on MLA citations the best print source is:

Gibaldi, Joseph. MLA Handbook for Writers of Research Papers. 6th ed. New York: MLA, 2003.

The Modern Language Association does not publish its documentation guidelines on the Web, however, the Purdue University Online Writing Lab website is a good online source for MLA guidelines: http://owl.english.purdue.edu/handouts/research/r_mla.html

In writing an MLA-style research paper, you must use in-text citations, set in parenthesis, to document your sources. Identify the source by the author and the page number. For example:

People from the Mediterranean prefer elbow-to-shoulder distance from each other (Smith 293).

If the electronic source has numbered paragraphs or sections instead of page numbers, use them for the parenthetical reference:

People from the Mediterranean prefer elbow-to-shoulder distance from each other (Smith, par. 7).

At the end of your paper, you must provide a list of your sources, with complete information, in a "Works Cited" section. In using MLA style to document your electronic sources, all references begin with the same information that would be provided for a printed source (or as much of that information as possible). The Web information is then placed at the end of the reference, after the access date. MLA style encloses Internet addresses and URLs (Uniform Resource Locators) in angle brackets < >. If you see them around an address, do not use them as part of the address when you attempt to retrieve the source.

See the Research Navigator homepage (www.researchnavigator.com) at the "End Notes & Bibliography" tab for guidance in setting up your MLA-style "Works Cited" section.

Chicago Manual Style (CMS) Guidelines

The fine arts and some fields in the humanities (but not literature) use traditional footnotes or endnotes, which should conform to standards set by *The Chicago Manual of Style* (CMS). The most recent (15th) edition of *The Chicago Manual of Style* includes general guidelines for citing electronic sources:

The Chicago Manual of Style, 15th ed. Chicago: University of Chicago Press, 2003.

The University of Chicago Press has a website you can use to research CMS style: http://www.chicagomanualofstyle.org

In the CMS system, you place superscript numerals within the text, like this.[15] Notes usually appear as footnotes; however, some instructors accept endnotes, in which notes all appear together at the end of the paper, not at the bottom of individual pages. There are two types of footnotes or endnotes: one documenting your sources with bibliographic information, the other discussing content-related matters.

If possible, use the footnote or endnote feature of your software; it will not only insert the raised superscript number in the text but also will keep your footnotes arranged properly at the bottom of every page or on a page at the end. It will also renumber your notes as you revise your paper.

In using CMS style to document your electronic sources, you should begin all references with the same information that would be provided for a printed source, and then identify the nature of the electronic source, give the date when the material was first cited or accessed, and provide an electronic address.

See the Research Navigator homepage (www.researchnavigator.com) at the "End Notes & Bibliography" tab for guidance in using CMS documentation.

Council of Science Editors (CSE) Style

CSE (Council of Science Editors, formerly the Council of Biology Editors) is a documentation style common in the health sciences, physics, mathematics, and other related disciplines. Within CSE style, there are three different formats for documentation: They are citation-name (C-N), citation-sequence (C-S), and name-year (N-Y). For more information on the newly revised (7th edition) of this style manual, visit the following link on the CSE website: http://www.councilscienceeditors.org/publications/style.cfm

See the Research Navigator homepage (www.researchnavigator.com) at the "End Notes & Bibliography" tab for guidance in using CSE documentation.

References

Chokshi, M., Carter, C., Gupta, D., Martin, T., & Allen, R. (1991). Computers and the apartheid regime in South Africa. *South Africa. Guide to Internet Resources.* Stanford University. Retrieved Dec. 12, 2002, from http://www-cs-students.stanford.edu/~cale/cs201

Goldstein, N. (Ed.). (1998) *The Associated Press Stylebook and Libel Manual.* Reading, MA: Addison-Wesley.

Halberstam, D. (2002, May 20). A Pultizer Prize-winner speaks of terrorism, life after college and choosing wisely. *USC Chronicle, 21*(29), 10-11.

Sollee, D. (2001). *Smart Marriages. The Coalition for Marriage, Family and Couples Education.* Retrieved December 12, 2002, from http://www.smartmarriages.com/divorcepredictor.html

Troyka, L.Q. (2007). *Simon & Schuster Handbook for Writers,* 8th ed. Upper Saddle River, NJ: Pearson Education.